salmonpoetry

Publishing Irish & International
Poetry Since 1981

D1612053

the arts council
an chomhairle ealaíon

funding
literature
artscouncil.ie

This is a collection of poems which comes at its ecological subject awry, never obviously, and there is humour as well as precision in the journeys these poems make and the subjects to which they attend. There are laments for extinct species, as well as endangered ones, but, with wit and imagination, these poems also commemorate and preserve 'extinct' female scientists: Rosalind Franklin, Marie Curie and Martha Maxwell, 'Mother of Taxidermy'. Moreover, in a collection of notable formal coherence – marine imagery ebbs and flows through it – this commitment to preservation can also be seen in the poetry's experimentation with formal shapes. These shapes are constraints or 'stiffners' as Robinson writes in 'Whalebone and Silk': 'Hooked, eyed and tight in my formal cocoon/no one can see me become a whale woman'. This is a formal impulse which can be seen most fully in 'Memories of Flight at the Life Museum', a crown of sonnets in darting short lines which really does take imaginative flight. Attentiveness to the precariousness of the natural world is matched, then, in *Journey to the Sleeping Whale*, by an equal attentiveness to language itself. Words here are:

> Vertebrae cast through the sandy deeps
> washed and tumbled and washed
> into fragments of meaning.

LEONTIA FLYNN

Citation as Judge of the 2019 Shine-Strong Award for Best First Collection

I read Jane Robinson's book with great joy. Poems like 'Building a Tower' and the poem of the whale woman, among others, are quite impressive. I like the combination of rhythms and assertions, the natural metaphors, the ecological sensibility, the intelligent back and forward between subjectivity and natural environment, the approach through senses to eco-political problems, the powerful symbols of the boats and navigations (ships full of animals in a very personal and feminist Noah's Ark). The book works very well as a whole, and the structure of the journey, through memory and sleep, also does. It is always a celebration to discover a new poet.

GERMÁN LABRADOR MÉNDEZ

Journey to the
Sleeping Whale

JANE ROBINSON

Winner of the 2019 Shine Strong Award
for Best First Collection

First Published in 2018 by
Salmon Poetry
Cliffs of Moher, County Clare, Ireland
This reprint published in 2020 by Salmon Poetry
Website: www.salmonpoetry.com
Email: info@salmonpoetry.com

ISBN 978-1-912561-37-7

Cover Artwork: *Bertie Pringle (image photographed by Paul Whelan)*
Cover Design & Typesetting: *Siobhán Hutson*

Printed in Ireland by Sprint Print

Salmon Poetry gratefully acknowledges the support of
The Arts Council / An Chomhairle Ealaíon

to my family

Acknowledgements

Acknowledgements are due to the editors of the following publications in which some of these poems first appeared:

Coast to Coast to Coast, the Four Corners Prize Anthology, the Hennessey New Irish Writing Page, The Stinging Fly, Science meets Poetry, The Abridged, Census, Can Can, Poetry Ireland Review, Human/Nature: Poems for Pacuare, Honest Ulsterman, The Interpreter's House, The Lion Tamer Dreams of Office Work, The Level Crossing, Magma, The Midir and Etain Anthology, Strokestown International Poetry Festival Website, Washing Windows? Irish Women Write Poetry and *Berryman's Fate: A Centenary Celebration in Verse.*

Thanks to Jessie Lendennie and Siobhán Hutson of Salmon Poetry for making the imagined book a reality, and to Bertie Pringle for the use of her painting.

Very special thanks to friends, fellow writers and my family for discussions, advice, inspiration and encouragement.

Contents

1

2

1

on the way out
high tide
cormorant on rock

Small Crustaceans

We could be drinking prism-split water,
licking the horizon, lapping at carrageen
fronds rimed by tiny crustaceans.

With lips salt-cracked and arms
burnt by the wind, the swell lifting

us out of our shells, we might seek
those lost at sea, or the fishes
composed of their spirits.

At Sea

In the chop and sulk of a North Atlantic swell,
with candle tallow, string and wool
to sew us into winter,

we round Hag's Head,
make anchor and eat stale bread,
row ashore to find a village shop

with cigarettes, perhaps a wilted cabbage,
feel our way across streaming hillsides,
build cairns on hummocks.

Horse Sound lies somewhere off the chart
obscured by low cloud.
Or is it graphite, chalk and soot?

On the Corner of Every Map is a Compass

The cartography of map fifty-six is blurred
until the rivers, rain-swollen, slide off
and into the printed sea. Those old roads
are less travelled than lines of coincidence
sketched on our faces. Sphagnum moss
would anyway have soaked your good leather
shoes on that verge by a ruined tower
where we might have sheltered, lost.

Fortune tellers map the hand's terrain,
grey toned roads begun in creased hollows.
Medicine, quick! Bring me medicine
for my heart, closed now, and aching
in the fine print, while I chase over Mullacor,
Giant's Cut, Lugduff, all the empty contours.

Meteorological Upset

Three starlings flew
through a hole

in the Arctic ice

and landed
on our washing line.

The Elusive

That cerulean blue
refuses to come,
won't paint itself

into these words.
The particular shade,
a faded denim sea-

washed, misted
out of landscape
photos, old women's

laundered blue dresses,
a door in a dream,
the glaze on a fish

or the rim of a bowl.
A most important blue,
the past almost

captured.

Baglady

Pictures fall from her collection,
coupons to the city's attractions
picked from carousels at the library.

James and the jaguar
look out with equal stares, heads
tilted together in her handbag's

cauldron. She might collect
doors into demolished houses,
from skips, if they fit in her bag.

She would construct into sculptures
cast-out wires and wood pallets
but her hands aren't strong enough

now, if they ever were. It is not
clothes or food she is after, it's the
makings of something more – gates

into elsewhere, a whole world
crumpled at the bottom of her bag
ready to be drawn out, transformed.

She wants to be a scholar

of the single stepped green shoot from a softened
piece of ginger in the kitchen,

of a knife cut in the maple board
and an unexpected lightness
at season's switch to colder weather,

of the empty stomach and an aromatic
feast, of climbing a heavy ladder to find
dust high in a roadside olive tree,

of how the Romans ate
every silphium-yielding plant
until they were extinct,

of the xerces blue and how to lever asphalt
from the earth
with a garden trowel,

of the shovel's heft and balance
on a bone fulcrum,

of how best to see
steam swirl from a mug of tea.

Lawn Care *etc.*

Watch me toss this quadrat on the grass,
catch the numbers in a square number game,
counting clover, cowslips, daisy plants
crammed, enclosed by a wooden frame.
But how random, really, was the quadrat toss,
angling my attention as I did, to bright blue?
Blue speedwell-eye drawing the square,
squarely down around itself, thrown true.
Truth is, this wasn't a scientific rectangle
tossed with the tosser's eye on the blue. But
frame the wild, who cares anymore to cram
plants in: mosses, dandelions? Stop your count-
game, we have weed-killed them all. Catch
grass and only grass inside the frame. Watch.

Mona Lisa

Bird flown through time: love child, magician,
magician's vision from the future, past.
Past master of volume and dimension,
dimension-traveller, who is it who spins so fast,
faster than the speed of anything known?

Known and unknown, everything's adventure,
adventurer, for you. Oh, frowning man,
man don't frown! Let rip the song and catch,
catch your thought before it vanishes.
In vanishing it leaves the crooked smile.

Crooked smile? See how she almost banished it,
banished the aviatrix grin, she is miles
and miles away, portrait of a vision.
Vision model twisted through from modern,
modern times, yes, to Leonardo's mind.

Leonardo's mind is sound box, echo chamber,
chambering each thought bounced back and forth,
back and forth: translation and transversion,
versions mirrored and reflected. His mouth?
His mouth is filled with beaks and wings of birds.

Muse Imperfected

She's pencilled on vellum,
fingertips marked with lead.
As she moves, graphite flows

over the paper, her hands drawn
across the neck of a viol. She
smells the bay leaves in her hair,

hears the strings vibrate, tastes
the artist's spit as he smudges
her pursed lips. Muse in Venice

who doesn't exist, she's paper
and pencil, shadows on snow,
downcast eyes listening for a note

of silence. Not flesh, no life
pulses in her veins because
she's drawn and I've torn it

again, ruined another good picture.
My blood mingled with her
anaemic fluids, sheet torn, milk

spilt, project abandoned on the table,
everything gone to the bad, a mind
lost in an instant, swallowed

by ghosts, the self left somewhere
beside a foreign road, dislocated,
enjambed, not making sense.

Adjustments may Lead to Disaster

After photo 365 by Chrissie White

A girl was bouncing,
got trapped in the moment,
her face misshapen by the camera flash,
her hair abandoned by gravity
over fabric sofa roses
printed long ago.

My Venetian pink pencil
rips open the wet paper,
a wound torn in the side
of the sepia print: seeping glue,
connective tissue, ruled lines,
cellulose, lymph.

Unable to restore now
any sense of vintage joy
to this picture, appropriated
and accidentally dissected, I watch
the girl tumble out of her dream
hit the floor hard.

Smog City Rhapsody

Ever been to your own wake, dancing in the dining room?
Out of the air to smog-hot streets, big cars purring
past the impossible afternoon bus-stop
waiting in refracted light, in post cards with palm trees
dungeon culture, all night talking...

    clever as a tunnel man
    fumbling and turning.

Rescued by the driver of a big yellow Chevy
drove it to the privy, smog city's bone-yard.
Flying and dancing with the damned
telephone wired to snowbound cities, manacled
to lily ponds. Science is an art for the go-ahead...

    crooked as a troubled man
    stumbling and turning.

    If you can feel the words written on your skin,
    if they won't come off, if they will never come off...

the weather comes and goes like static on the radio.
Ever been stopped, striding wet cheeked, awful
by a man in a silver bullet, said, you are beautiful...
did he mean the cry for him
dreaming ghosts in the drip?

    Mortal as a healer man
    tumbling and turning.

Strung out on neural circuits – exile sorrow,
electrical – all night, late night, every night
bicycle past the black dog attack,
freeway bridge vertigo,
sweet apricot garden, a glut of sugar globes,

careful as a Rasta man
spelling and turning.

If in a clean season, a wanderer,
if on a blue clock, the numbers collect on one side
if they've forgotten how to say your name
– pale face, sunshine, no bloom on the cheeks –
if in a restaurant eating noodles
if it is a crowd of blank faces
if not then… but now.

Student

Dimmed in smog of L A
singing the freeway bridge blues,
the wrapped-toffee river of cars

cutting through memories,
orange groves, live oaks,
chaparral. Blood of coyotes

pierced by inventions, bright
men exploding atoms
or the next great idea.

Her shades insufficient
to shrivel the glare of history,
or was it industry, taking life,

taking on shape, machine-
driven, bulging with pistons,
circuits, the whole business.

Watching a movie of sunsets
reflected from particles:
glossed in, unable to shout.

She had felt as though
in a greenhouse, impossibly
large, unpeeling rose-tinted

beauty. Experiments
leap-frogging one on another,
shining P-thirty two

on cold film, method lately
abandoned because of its danger
to fish in the drains,

the odd alligator.
She had felt like a wallet
left out in the weather, notes,

lips stuck together, fading
identity nibbled and bent.
Bivouacked in the desert,

she had only one vision,
a ghost-ridden motorbike,
roaring unheard through the night.

The Nights are Long Now

The spider took me and she spun me in her web,
tent pegs through the heart,
a bite on the thigh numbing my foot.
I fell from the bed,

feet tangled in my winding sheet of silk,
mouth papered over with moth wings.
I forgot to listen
when the owl called my name.

Radium Mother, 1903

Marie Curie's cookery book
is so radioactive, they say,
it must be locked in a lead box:

we should wear protective clothes —
white bodyalls, helmet-mask,
lead gloves — to open it and see

the garlic stains, soup splashes,
crushed and stirred and served
by her glow-in-the-dark hands.

And *This* Madness

The Trinity Test, 1945

Fire heads held in our hands,
wearing shades we lie poolside
in dry-land, sip soda from straws,
ringside view, *Journey of Death*
where we're about to implode

the gadget. Excited, we wait,
euphoric, for explosion.
Lift the tops off our heads!
Blow us away – jaded
as we are, insipid – pinned

to our deck chairs, eyes sinking
in hot sand, hungry for neon
power, Las Vegas.
Jumping hand-in-hand into pools
of deep nowhere, atom absorbed,

these lunatic hands taking bets
on the planet's survival.
We are swimming through blast,
bronzed torsos burnt, sunglasses
swirling somewhere in fallout.

Our game faces stitched, painted
respectable masks, puppets
mindless now, wooden string strung
crawling appalled in the bad lands,
sipping from poisonous springs.

Postcard

Not doing so well
in this chocolate place
of pink fluorescent haloed saints,
my breastplate
enamelled like a mystery by Paul Klee,
the blue grid
of my robot heart's buttons
pressable. While you,
you are distant,
indifferent.

Multiple Exposures

*In memory of Rosalind
Franklin (1920-1958)*

There's a photo of Rosalind
elegant and happy in a Parisian dress.
She strolls across the laboratory,

a ceramic crucible in each hand,
and offers coffee to her friends.
Another photograph shows Rosalind

bent over her microscope, arranging
DNA and focusing the beam
which carries on through her labcoat.

In a basement in postwar London no one
was careful to limit her exposure time.
Here's Photo 51 by Rosalind –

*the most beautiful x-ray photograph
of any substance ever taken* –
a colleague brought it up from her lab

and showed it to his friends.
She left to work somewhere else.
Airbrushed out of the photo. Rosalind's
skirt suddenly tight under her labcoat.

Martha Maxwell, Mother of Taxidermy

Have you put her body onto the page
nicks and cuts on each hand
the scraping blade,
train vibrations driving up from the sacrum?

All the crystal eyes
held and turned and painted,
the exactness of paint flecks, she licking
a sable tip, yellow and red cadmiums

crossing her tongue.
These softened furs stroked and handled,
she knowing where each was shot,
their bodies left among rocks; for vultures

will come down into her inventions,
theatre of the wild.
Is she in these padded places,
angularities of elbows, boots buttoned

to the knees, dress closed
at the throat, her tight swallowing?
Not mittelschmerz but a flowering of cells,
a hand pressed.

Materials Required

Gun,
neatsfoot oil from shinbones and feet but not the hooves,
an inflorescence of blue,
broken hacksaw blade,
the stitching finger,
strontium yellow or barium yellow,
massicot mixed with sugar candy,
formaldehyde,
luck.

Memories of Flight at the Life Museum

Archways hold the memory of bones
and the floors are worn –
look up and see the whale frames,
all blubber gone,
afloat from chains,
swimming through museum dust,
singing their own silent songs:
big and black and secret.
But they're old and dead and our necks
are getting cricks
from looking up,
so we look down
and away to the side, avoiding the gaze
of the endangered whales.

ii

Of the endangered whales
there are many in this room,
invited in through the escape hatch
and into
the house,
its walls pressing against their sides.
Out of their element, beached, fouled
in blankets, sheets, unable to find
her in her dreams, she's drifted so,
so far out to sea.
Under the blue, in the blue,
of so much blue it's hard to be
intelligent any more, awake, grown
wary of the dark and all it shows.

iii

Wary of the dark and all it has shown,
electrocuted by putting a hand
into the kettle after turning it on –
a sparkle-band
crackling,
the buzz at the back
rising up from the neck,
electric.
After the excursion, fall asleep on the boat,
lulled by ocean-crossing swells,
a scent of seaweed in the hold.
Another disaster
avoided. Or was it the chance to fly, failed:
the bird swapping her feathers for scales?

iv

The bird, swapping her feathers for scales,
said, 'look at me now,
now that my feathers have grown so small,
and scaly enough for a fish or a coelacanth.
Look at me swim!'
And (though the sea was cold)
she plunged in,
closing her eyes as the dream took hold.
It was dark in the deeps
and the fish grew a lamp
to light her phosphorescent way, to creep
through seaweeds of the underneath.
Now, pushed and washed, we come to the coastal fish,
white and gloomy in blue-glass cubes.

v

White and gloomy, held in blue glass. Cube-
shaped tanks hold the bleached
bodies of two poor cod
caught (Dublin Bay, 1888)
and arranged beside pouting, four bearded rockling,
spear-snouted grenadier, silvery pout
and Ekstrom's topknot;
all trapped in their tanks, not looking out.
Fish grown white in their frames,
grown abstract as people
strange in the head, games
so weird
we want to go up the forbidden stairs
and laugh among the formaldehyde jars.

vi

Laughing among the formaldehyde jars,
the dissection kits and scalpels;
dosing ourselves at the bars.
With a knife in hand, the surgeon is gentle
and reconstructs the inner ear
so we can hear
even the sound
of an owl
landing on her feathered feet,
and smell
the cheap
stink of jumbo-jet fuel
from two miles down, pinned to the ground
like rabbits frozen in mid-bound.

vii

Like rabbits, frozen in mid-bound,
frozen under the car's lights,
picked out
in terrible bright
detail. The driver slams
on her brakes.
The dreamer awakes
with a bang,
the zoom and fright
of a light aircraft going down,
the sieze and roar of its engines in the night,
blazing out of the sky, struts and compass gone.
And suddenly we're all brought down,
dead cubs curled at the feet of a trophy lion.

viii

Dead cubs curled at the feet of a trophy lion
(Dublin Zoo, 1894)
starving and cold in the big museum.
Lucky we can't hear the laughing roar,
lucky for us the spotted hyaena
is a big dream
as he looms in the next glass case,
blood and guts all over his face.
And hear the little girl cry, 'that is a scary
hippo
for me, Mama. Mama, that hippo
is looking at me.'
We wander on, through the afternoon blur,
watching clothes moths dine on the dried-up fur.

ix

Clothes moths dine on the dried-up fur,
and tied to the foot of every mammal
there is a label
stating – date collected, and by which person.
From the forbidden balcony
all the gazelles of the world look down,
or around,
as though stretching their necks through the wall,
as though stabled up there
instead of dead in some far off Africa,
where
(leaving the bodies for vultures)
Victorian hunters once shot their claim
of the extinct and the in-danger.

x

Of the extinct and the endangered
blue-throated ones, choking –
I'd hold their throats
if I could, range
over time, backwards
to then
and forwards
to what might be, tomorrow, again.
Spix's macaw, dead in captivity, three specimens;
Sharpe's rail (Leiden museum, 1865), extinct.
I'd cradle their heads
in my hands
and hold their throats so they couldn't join
the greatest marsupial carnivore, dead.

xi

Thylacine, largest marsupial carnivore:
ugly dog,
extinct dog,
pouched, bagged and gone.
It could be warfarin in the wood shed,
a witch's apple,
make even the crows and the rats play dead
with only a local ripple.
Does it have to be so final,
why not sleep, Kumbhakarna, sleep,
until you find,
one day, the strength to wake.
Wake and listen to an owl whisper in your ear
you hear... you hear... you hear...

xii

You hear, it will get better
though the books look like too-sweet sweets,
chocolates in their metallic wrappers,
much too much. A surfeit
of all that once pleased your beautiful
mind,
the animal inside.
Burnt out... patched, stretched and glued –
the African yellow-winged bat,
but why this one, why not that?
It's something about the repaired wings held
at the angle of about-to-dive, yet
still looking up. Still ready to try
another flight.

xiii

Another flight –
and it's the voice of Amelia Earhart
on the air,
KHAQQ calling Itaska,
we are on the line
one five seven, three three seven,
KHAQQ to Itaska, we are running on the line, North
and South.
All the remains: bone-handled double-
bladed jackknife,
hand lotion bottle,
woman's compact.
The voice, low and sweet and reasonable –
but was there a hint of fear?

xiv

There was a hint of fear
about ditching on an uninhabited island,
about making it an uninhabited island
by eating
all the dodos
(none of those
at the Dublin
museum, and the specimen in London
has two left feet
collected so long ago, after the Arnhem's crew,
shipwrecked, 1662,
had eaten the meat.)
Many years after she went down, they found only
bits of metal, some glass, and no bones.

xv

The archways smelt of bones,
and the endangered whales.
We walked through the dark and all it shows:
birds who swapped feathers for scales
gone gloomy into the blue,
friends laughing and jarred,
frozen rodents
curled at the feet of cars.
Clothes moths dined on furs
of the extinct and the in-danger,
they ate the last of the marsupial carnivores,
you hear. But now, hear the strange
other flight –
beyond bones and fear, a hint of light?

Conservation Status, Vulnerable

Leatherback turtle
sucks down the pale, moon-shaped
plastic bag.

Under Sail

My father, asleep, far out at sea
with his tiller fixed to a course,
sailed into a sleeping whale

who gently submerged,
chose not to thrash her tail
or scupper the homemade boat.

2

on the way home
ebbing tide
heron on rock

Rana temporaria is Ireland's Only Frog

i   Inside – Outside

There's stuff going down the drain
we'd be mad to drink (think detergent,

bleach, fluorescent brightener)
and somewhere near the outfall,

a frog
whose skin's a mucous membrane

like my eyes and mouth,
where inside opens wetly to the outside.

ii   Origami Frog

The brown paper square folds into frog
in all her damp skin, gold-dotted,
wild with grass and water, caught
by one leg in a heron's beak or trapped
two handed and dissected, scored
open with a scalpel, undressed,
skin stretched and pulled apart,
pinned on a maroon-dark tray of wax.

As the live frog's lustre dulls,
we struggle to cram it all back in,
refold skin over stomach and nerves,
stitch her up, preserve the species –
thumb-smoothed, rubbed and stroked
to a thin and slippery tissue ghost.

iii   Infinity = Tadpole

<pre>
                    pond
              pond frog pond
         pond frog   frog pond
       pond frog   frog pond
      pond frog   frog pond
    pond frog   frog pond
    pond frog   frog pond
  pond frog   ∞   frog pond
    pond frog   frog pond
    pond frog   frog pond
      pond frog   frog pond
       pond frog   frog pond
         pond frog   frog pond
              pond frog pond
                    pond
</pre>

47

Those who were Seen Dancing

We've rolled up our sleeves. Our ears
feel too warm. We are not insane
but glow with more images to see,
so much to conjure into picture-music;
and we observe each day the dance
of light and dark across our limbs, these

long lucid journeys into dream, this
scratch of ballpoint over pages. Hear
the paper's texture as the pigment dances
line by line? The order keeps us sane
and if we midnight-listen, the music
of dreamt words paints a truer scene

though it might be upside-down, seem
inside-out or strange, we'll find those
puzzles will unravel into future music.
Odd, how some of the things we hear
while running full-tilt may seem insanely
like a fortune teller's words, dancing

out new truths before we know the dance.
And when, asleep, I plunge into the sea
the cold will shock my heart (its insane
pounding out of sync) and, praying these
won't be my last few moments, I'll hear,
from far away, a most enticing music.

Is it this yearning for an unknown music
keeps us tuned up, longing for the dance
although the rust already has set in? Hear
the rhythm of infinity: can you see
predictive patterns, can you feel these
beauty traces, the tree of life's insane

bloom? Then comes a falling away, sanity
questioned, limp-limbed, unmoved by music
which plays in some distant room, these
grapes uneaten, days darkened, the dance
faltering a bit. But there's light still, see?
Come closer now, I'll whisper in your ear

about the day we saw those people dancing
in the street, insanely, to a silent music. Picture
us again, weeping for a beat we couldn't hear.

Song of the Paper Nest

I'm an open
mouth, an o,
an act of beauty.
She draws me down
layer by layer,
a phallic egg
glued to the porch beam
with paper and spit.
Moulded by mandible
and stick-leg,
the ingress
this mouth hole,
open to the world
and singing.

Ex-Libris

I'm at the bookshop now, solace
impossible at the bottom of a box
squashed under other volumes,
displaced. I miss my place
in her library calm and dusted,

rubbing covers with a hundred
others: their silver-tongued gossip,
print vibrating its molecules,
ink-atoms dry but driven, proton-
quick electron, the spinning

heart of the matter, my fellow
volumes loud even on the shelf.
My mistress elegant, immaculate,
running her ringed fingers over
our spines, choosing by Braille:

smudging sun-struck edges,
caressing covers, sniffing at
pages as if she would eat us.
She's chosen me, fresh and tight,
many nights more than the others,

slipped her fingers under
my covers, never bumped my tips -
skylarks have flown all over
her sheets, fluttered at windows.
Recently too austere in my pale

blue covers, linen spine… I'm
ready to be dog-eared, foxed,
tossed in a green bag with notes,
books, pens. Ready to be taken
apart, my small explosions

pondered, continued. I admit
to being shaken now, my end-
papers chipped. How I long
for a person to carry me up, open
my body, let sparrow-hawks out.

Elegy for a Meadow

All of your fragments: unfinished, fallen,
discarded like letters lost in a field
dug down by worms, driven under:

ploughed over, mown green, gathered up,
swept off and tweezed out, superseded,
wrapped in black plastic, baled and tucked.

The silage sewing up seeds, eggs, cocoons,
boiling embryonic plants and unformed songs
cramped in fermentation's fetid, hot rot

where corncrakes and cowslips have gone,
the meadow pipits' nests parcelled together
with meadow brown larvae and meadowsweet seeds.

We scatter patterns from packeted fields
but this gap between now and the next extension
may be too small, may not hold birds and insects.

Do we grasp at dead images: melted wax
seals from old letters, bright welted blossoms
excavated, unfurled, almost butterfly-tongued?

Why do we do this?

It hurts me
on the apex of the tragus
right below the supratragic notch –
those diamond drill bits,
oil wells, water wells, oil wells
driven deep through subcutaneous
limestone – it pierces to the bone.

I'd remove
the hard metallic studs
and salve her wounds with comfrey,
heal-all, knapweed
stew hyssop with wild strawberries,
feed the birds
and teach them how to speak.

Peace Treaty

'All fish-weirs shall be removed…'
Magna Carta, 1215

Come, step into the disused water meadow
overgrown by water mint and meadowsweet.
We'll write our vows of peace in oak-gall ink
on lime-white parchment near the great yew tree.
Let no fears foreshadow
the next eight hundred years held in a hollow
quill from the goose or the swan's left wing. But link

forwards from then to the phosphor screen and plastic
key. Hear that we still must dismantle those weirs,
unravel the gill-nets, ban echo-locators, allow
fish and more for every person, otter and heron. No fear,
no war, no silver bombers, harriers. Let fly the larks
trapped under our scarves
to sing for peace – in eight hundred years, and now.

At the Seaside

Where are they, those tables,
    the vertebrae
    of whales washed up
    on Ballynamona strand?

And where are the knives
    we used to find,
    razor sharp shells
    black-blue strewn by the sea?

And where are our plates,
    oysters pearl-
    glazed, carefully placed
    with seaweed meals?

All eaten. In our sleep we have eaten
    the tables,
    the knives
    and the plates.

Beast of the Sea

Recumbent on the kitchen floor,
seeking krill with my open mouth
but finding only crumbs

and dust and shopping lists,
my big whale of a body
longing for salt sea buoyancy

the skeleton's sockets and joints
covered in blubber,
stretched mouth echoing the ocean.

Asleep on the surface,
or plunging and wallowing,
at play with the scales of fish.

Vertebrae cast through sandy deeps
washed and tumbled and washed
into fragments of meaning.

All the lemons we have eaten

from my palm I smell
the golden fruit, an orchard sharp
with bee-hum and birds

imagine how bitter
the taste of lemons
from poisoned groves

on the tide-line a tiny yellow net
as for its lemons
we ate them when we were young

at the factory they grow
gardens in the dark — citric acid
from *Aspergillus*

Sketch Map of a Temporary Wilderness

Development lands, Luas Green Line
   – Sandyford to Cherrywood

To enter you'll pass fifteen bees feeding on ivy flowers,
scramble a steep mud mound blocking the gate
and dry your mouth on unripe sloes.

Sketch a map with charcoal from a clear-felled willow copse –
stones, road, hill, high cross, dolmen, open space.
All field names have been forgotten.

I eat handfuls of seedy blackberries, purple my fugitive map
with their juice. The eye in the sky doesn't see rabbits
track through the spinny

where a fox has scattered pigeon down, the river
loud as it enters the woods. Beside the ravine –
graffiti, aerosol cans, barbed-wire tangles.

Someone's garden, someone's abandoned building site,
a city planner's projection map, everyone's ride
at the speed of light.

When Building a Tower

While the jack-hammer stabs the granite,
a hard rattle far below, the day falls
away, away in a jackdaw's spread wings.

Hard-hat plastic curves in yellow,
ears fill with the lilting buzz of Babel.
Dropped by a crane, flight is possible

but won't let slow the beating heart,
won't let go the night, and some birds spiral
the enamel sky, the scaffold boards.

Behind smoked glass of a square mask,
tacking steel beams with molten metal,
arms lifted all day to knock off flux...

through sinew, muscle, ultraviolet skin –
the shoulders ache, and there it tumbles,
a feathered one, shaken and barbed.

A Game of Fidchell

After the Ballinderry Game Board
and the legend of Midir and Étain

On the hill we lean to each other, you
take the woman's head on your knee, I
her feet. At play we become one husband –
oak limbs melded, bodies lost as we dice

for your wife, my wife, the butterfly.
On an oracle board we could lose our minds
to the game. You move with care and I by whim
on a seven times seven grid. Erratic winds

blow our golden balls from well to dark well.
You peg them down for a forest, fully grown,
and a road over the bog. My breath swells
while my heart roils like the fetch from a rogue

wave and I win the third game with no effort.
She and I become one pure spirit, feathered.

First Long Journey

The bowl envies the golden moon
as I envy the haptic spread of painted
ink, meaning everything and nothing.
Not needing to signify but to induce

a sensation where one's feet might leave
the ground for a few seconds, long enough
to give the floaty feeling of a dream
where the dreamer flies downstairs
toes not quite bumping on the steps.
And here's the push from underneath:

black, apparent ground, which could be
the blackness of a hole like the rows
of little holes our daughter, one year old,
couldn't help exploring on the train.

Lament for an Extinct Species

Benjamin, last Thylacine,
died Hobart Zoo, 1936

i

The mercury sank
lower than ever when Benjamin,
last thylacine,
locked out at night, died.

It was a forgotten event,
no bones or pelt kept.
Regret is 3 minutes, 9 seconds,
of silent film footage.

Once carved into Ubirr rocks,
we scratch his image onto paper.
These are relics – skeletons
a museum bought from bounty hunters

back when the species declined
and relatives died
in cages all over Europe,
neglected, unbred.

ii

& how do we grieve for a species?
One woman went a bit mad,

tried to conjure the thylacine back,
nurture ghost whelps at the breast.

On her bra rose-petal stains remain
from the pink rose petals

she tucked in like tiny shell bodies
of marsupial pups in the pouch.

iii

I come to this discipline in rage,
looking for a voice to sing me as
deep as the whales. I come with
the weight of a thousand books on
my back, asking it to release me
into my own body. I come in despair,
looking for images to rose-tint my
eyes and flow out of my mouth.
To this discipline, begging for wisdom
to utter the word *extinction*, I come.

iv

the bags were then opened, and pieces of glass and shells taken out
dolor, dolas, tasa, murhe, brón, buairt,
there can be no consolation,

with which they lacerated their thighs, backs, and breasts
ochón is ochón, rope, jad, jale, tuga,
there can be no comfort,

in a most frightful manner, whilst the blood kept pouring out of the wounds
ag, weh, malheur, gofid, grief, luctu,
there can be no remedy,

in streams… continuing their wild and piercing lamentations
suru, sorrow, sorg, iefgray, orrowsay,
there can be no salvage,

there can be no salvage,
there can be no remedy,
there can be no comfort,
there can be no consolation.

the bags are again opened, and pieces of glass and shells taken out

The Empty Spaces

There is no space
between these pebbles
jumbled together,
each one contacting
several others,
washed up
onto the ramparts
of the sea wall.

Only when we
pick with deliberating
fingers, special stones
from among the scraps
of broken glass
and plain stones,
do we get something
to arrange on the page,
something that allows
spaces to intervene.

Today I have made
a collection of terrible
masks: *The Scream*,
an elephant-headed monster,
a pocked monkey head.
The spaces between them
are mistakes we have made,
the stones shouting
about what we might
have done differently.

Painting the Bedroom

At an angle of falling out of the window,
I'm blooded
with ink stains and splashed paint.
The ladder-craft needed to climb this wall
has given so much trouble, aspiring
to heaven. Brush stretched up, shaft
clutched in cramped fingers,
I suck in, breath by breath, smoke
and dust in Brownian motion.
Twice I've dreamed of us at sea,
on a ferryboat sunk on the journey.
When living feels like too much work

it is dangerous to lean out of the bed,
maybe fall from your body on the next bend.

At the Stop Sign

On a day like today, with rain
pouring down the windscreen, not
much visible beyond the next car, rain
gathered in puddles by the curb and rain-
water lapping the toes of peoples' boots
when they try a longstep to avoid the puddled rain
and with one foot trembling over flooded drains
they seem to catch their breath
and float out from the pavement – breathing
air mixed fifty-percent with rain –
until they reach the other side and click
their heels back down on the road, they click

their fingers at the leap, and click,
clock, off they go through a veil of rain…
Dreaming at the wheel again, the click
of wipers awakens the driver and she clicks
into action, brain empty, nothing
there but the automated click
of changing gears and revving up, the clicking
accelerator pressed by her boot –
one toe-nail turned black from wearing those boots
a little too tight – and that's when it finally clicks:
his photos were taken right here… she breathes
in and out more slowly now, each breath

measured as she tries to breathe
her way back to the day when she clicked
open the briefcase lock with a screwdriver, breath
held in case she should find some breath
of the past left behind, perhaps a rain-
spotted note or brass compass breathing
out a faint scent of the sea. But the length and breadth
of his briefcase had been emptied, there was nothing
left, except two photographs of nothing
known. The lid drifted down, exuding a breath
of mothballs while she studied the red boots
of the woman in the photos, her boots

so bright she seemed to float, red boots
gliding three inches at least, or the breadth
of a hand, above the pavement. Those boots
red against grey, an unknown woman in boots
striding along with a clickety click.
As in a diptych, the high-heeled boots
daubed a red spot, drawing the eyes. Boots
crisp against the blurred grey of rain-
drenched cement and fence. Roadside and rain
a background to the day, the scent of those boots
step, stepping their way in two old photos, nothing
to tell her name, or the name of that place, not

a clue about why she was there, nothing
but the set of her shoulders and those red boots.
The oval blur of her face as she caught his eye, no
ties to the future or the past, nothing
now will tell us her name. A breath
of wind shakes heavy drops down and none
of it makes sense any more, nothing
but two blurred photos hastily clicked
from a car, as though the scene clicked
and he wanted to make something out of nothing.
And now, there is more rain
pouring down the windscreen, enough rain

to drench his photo-woman who had drops of rain
sparkling on her shoulders, or mist, or nothing –
its hard to tell at this distance – the red boots
dancing across the page and no breath
on his windscreen, while these wipers continue to click.

Lines for a Rescue

All night she's watched and re-watched him climb the indistinct, thin branches of a tree filmed near Amsterdam. As she puts herself into the lacework of his tree she forgets to breathe. Hold tight, don't jump! Breathe, don't drown! Is this ache-all-over-the-body some kind of dying? Is this forgetting-to-breathe the false calm of nervous systems shutting down?

> *In the film, Jan jumps into the canal – his hand lets go that last branch, twigs snap, t-shirt billows and he falls, falling forever in grey-tone, face turned aside.*

Libations of ink and milk, and seaweed hand-picked off stones where they found Jan's boat, half underwater, with him aged thirty-three lost at sea while in search of the miraculous – alone, on a 12-foot boat, sailing from a torch-lit night in LA to the lighthouse of home. Pitfall predicted.

> *It plays in her head – when he reached for the boat it had drifted, waves washed his face and the stars dimmed like lights seen through rain when the wipers break.*

She's kept watch too late, trying to guess why she sketched his jump, scumbled his body, painted his boat underwater. Obsessed. Collaged seas into currents and surges, laid thick ochre ropes like blood hawsers. It is physics, gravity, physical perfections holding us up. Does it all come down to the tree-branched nature of life, dreams, decision points, divinations?

> *From the camera, no last shot of his fall from the boat, no picture of his grab for the line, but these lines. Many years later, a link – miracle almost perceived.*

On Waking

Immobile as a moth
wound in spider silk.
Recumbent, hazed about
with bliss, a fog of it
still over the glass
lake at dawn, liquid
as nothing ever was.
Replete with nothingness
a bright shiver
from brain to toe tips
and if that, before, was
the little death, this
must be the big one.

Secondhand Smoke

If you've ever loved a smoker you'll remember
that last cigarette stubbed out
on the station platform and, in spite of all

the smoke that choked you over table after table,
you'll steal a cigarette from your mother
and creep out behind the fence like a teenager.

You've been longing for this smoke for years now
but you fumble the matchbox in the dark
and all the little matchsticks fall down among

long grass stems, nettles sting your hand,
so you go inside and drink a cup of tea,
the stolen cigarette in your pocket's already limp

and crushed, maybe you should have taken two.
You did take two because you imagined
this before it happened. If you ever loved

a smoker you might have asked his brother
to join you behind the tennis court and smoke
the two crushed cigarettes together, share

the harsh and tender smoke from mouth to mouth.
As it turns out, you have swiped three smokes
because you planned it all, including

your own private smoke among the nettles
behind the shed, in the morning when everyone
is out, when you don't drop the matches

and light with trembling fingers an adventure
into someone else's mind. The bit you didn't plan
was that he'd be right here behind the shed

with you, inside your head, all the way,
as you drag in the smoke and smoke your first
and only cigarettes, thirteen years too late.

Whalebone and Silk

Apology to <u>Eubalaena glacialis</u>,
good whale of the ice.

A shortage of breath brought on
by compression of my collapsible ribs
under your mouthparts, strongly
moulding my waist and padded hips,
pressing upwards on my small breasts.
Fingers fumble to undo my tight-laced
bodice, release this whalebone cleavage.
Unwound and harpooned I faint,
fall into the silk moths' boiling pot,
into the North Sea turmoil of your flensing.
Baleena, Baleena, forgive me! I forgot,
no I never knew, how they got these stiffeners.
Hooked, eyed and tight in my formal cocoon,
no-one can see me become a whale woman.

Single-handed

My boat's
been at sea so long
I'm starving, can't eat these
sandwiches pinned to my sleeve,
cucumbers over my eyes.

What's in your pocket?
Holly-berry, hook and line,
a folded car in the shape of a whale.
In archaeological terms, no magic coin
and in the heart of the sea – the turtle, this box.

We will be luminous
in our tattered gear, boating across oceans
where our lips afford the sweetest tasting.
Such thirst our tongues, like foreign bodies,
clank against our teeth.

Though the sea
hides most of our secrets
nobody sits in the white plastic chair
on the jetty you'll find
at 11° 35' N 165° 23' E.

My boat of bird feathers
withstood many sharks
but today it leaks inexplicably.
An octopus wrapped herself round the windlass,
she changes colour before we go down.

Running Repairs

To repair the ship I pray –
my father returns from a grave sleep

with webs from the spiders met on his way
and glue from the parachute beetles.

Tacking fabric together
in the hot lagoon of a Pacific atoll

we'll patch this hole with gossamer,
salt and blue rose petals.

Unfamiliar Territory

Night falls like octopus ink over xeroxed streets.
I light my candle and run through alleyways

searching for the compass rose, the smell of home
or a dry crust of bread to eat with these sweet figs.

I've ruined the map, marching over ancient villas,
splashing through marshes. I lost my left shoe

in Piano, my senses at the Hill of Ants. Brain
scrambled by lines and details, places with no

meaning. Maze-like, these dark roads lead nowhere
until I find a river and, remembering that water

must flow down to water, launch a leaf boat
and cram myself in, balanced grimly on the rib.

I set such wispy, spider-web sails you wouldn't
believe escape possible from this precarious muddle.

After 10

For this performance she lies on bare bedsprings,
mortal with the *thinky death*.
Henry's gagged and bound in orange string.
Sailed a boat whose wood had rotted,
snapped mast wrapped in stays, rudder stowed
under a henhouse. They peck

and worry old boxes of paper.
She's plaintive, restless, the doctor
left long ago. Imaginary bones being no
replacement. And the others afraid of the jackdaw
(coat thrown
over the cage, pull of her finger-fed beak)

they left too. Like riding a bike,
you don't forget. She's sunk, so hopeless
she might try again, sort through those stones
one more time. *Is there anybody out there?*
Friend's missing – stage right, no one – nowhere.
Progressive deterioration, he liked.

Picture us Again

Come closer now, I'll whisper in your ear
about the day we saw those people dancing

in the street, insanely, to a silent music. Picture
us again, weeping for a beat we couldn't hear.

Notes

On the Corner of Every Map is a Compass – The central area of the Wicklow Mountains is covered by O.S. Map 56.

Lawn Care etc. – A quadrat is a square frame used by ecologists to mark out a standard unit of area, selected at random, for studying the distribution of species over a larger area.

Muse Imperfected – Interaction with a pencil drawing, *Cassandra Fedele* by F. W. Burton, National Gallery of Ireland.

And This *Madness* – The Trinity Test was the first detonation of a nuclear device, and took place in the *Jornada del Muerto* desert of New Mexico, USA.

Multiple Exposures – Rosalind Franklin's independent labwork helped Watson & Crick develop their theory of DNA structure. The quotation in italics is from J. D. Bernal. Franklin died of ovarian cancer, probably as the result of x-ray exposure during her experiments.

Martha Maxwell, Mother of Taxidermy – Martha Maxwell (1831-1881), a naturalist and artist from Colorado, is credited with inventing taxidermy and the museum diorama.

Memories of Flight at the Life Museum – Refers to the Natural History Museum in Dublin, and to imagined elsewhere.

Rana temporaria is Ireland's Only Frog – 42 percent of the world's 6,000 frog species are declining rapidly and are in danger of extinction in our lifetime. Since 1980, 122 amphibian species are thought to have gone extinct, compared to just five bird species and no mammals over the same period... Smithsonian Conservation Biology Institute.

Those who were Seen Dancing – End words from F. Nietzche: *Those who were seen dancing were thought to be insane by those who could not hear the music*.

Why do we do this? – Hyssop was used by Hildegard of Bingen to treat melancholy.

Lament for an Extinct Species – Italics in Section iv quoted from a description in Edward Eyre's (1840-1) *Journal of Expeditions*. The thylacine's closest living relatives, the numbat and the Tasmanian devil, are both now endangered.

First Long Journey – Describes a painting, *Still Life in Purple* by Patrick Hickey, at the Irish Writers' Centre.

The Empty Spaces – Refers to *Der Schrei der Natur* (The Scream of Nature) by Edvard Munch, and written in an attempt to explore the Japanese concept of *Ma*, or Negative Space.

Lines for a Rescue – In memory of, and after the life's work of, conceptual artist Bas Jan Ader (1942-1975)

Whalebone and Silk – Apology to the whale, after an X-ray photograph of the torso of a woman in a whalebone corset made of silk stiffened with strips of bristle, known as whalebone, from the mouths of baleen whales. The North Atlantic right whale, *Eubalaena glacialis*, is on the IUCN Red List of endangered species.

Single-handed – The map coordinates are for Bikini Atoll, atomic test site.

After 10 – Quotations in italics from John Berryman's *Dreamsong 10* and Pink Floyd's *The Wall*.

JANE ROBINSON grew up in Ireland and worked abroad, in the USA and India, for twenty years. Informed by a BA from Trinity College Dublin and a PhD in Biological Science from the California Institute of Technology, much of her writing would now be described as ecopoetry. Poems from this, her first, collection have won the Strokestown International Poetry Prize and the Red Line Book Festival Poetry Award; were second for the Patrick Kavanagh Poetry Award; and have been commended for a variety of awards including the Oxford Brookes International Poetry Competition and the Pacuare Poetry Competition in support of Pacuare Reserve, a conservation initiative based in Costa Rica. Jane lives in Dublin with her husband and their two daughters.

www.salmonpoetry.com

"Like the sea-run Steelhead salmon that thrashes upstream to its spawning ground, then instead of dying, returns to the sea – Salmon Poetry Press brings precious cargo to both Ireland and America in the poetry it publishes, then carries that select work to its readership against incalculable odds."